EDUCATORS SUCCESS STORIES

DR DHEERAJ MEHROTRA DR R K DAS

Contents

Preface

Educators Success Stories is a quality initiative by RKDx Talks. The purpose is to showcase the wonderful personalities who have had the sharing of their talks and deliberations during and post corona period with an emphasis on quality education and delivery.

The platform figured out these innovative and creative educators who not only shared their skills via practice but also made the scenario bolder with the adoption of technology in a big way.

We at RKDx Talks salute these noble educators and wish them luck in future.

Authors

CHAPTER I

Success Stories

RKDX TALKS is a Global RK Quotes Speakers Forum unit registered under the Ministry of MSME Govt of India and ISO (9001:2015) Certified. RKDx TALKS is one of the leading international virtual speakers platforms for School Leaders, Principals, Vice Principals, Coordinators and Educators.

Dr RK Das starts the talk show in the year 2021 & the main objective is to inspire and live during the most challenging days (Pandemic). We are excited to list some educators with their success stories as a mark of recognition.

• • •

• • •

• • •

• • •

• • •

• • •

Story #1

Dr Ishtiyaque Ahmed Shaikh

Gender

Answer: Male

Designation & Name of School or institution

Answer: Principal, Vishwakarma Empros International School, Talegaon, Pune, Maharashtra, India

Mobile Number (Whatsapp)

Answer: 9370364759

Write about your Achievement and experience in about 250 words

Answer: Let's Learn by Doing.'Learning is a process whereby learning is created through the transformation of experience. '

To encourage interest in social studies and provide an opportunity for "learning by doing", an insightful activity was conducted for grade 9th students. Dr Istiyaque Ahmed Shaikh, the

Principal, took the students on the open ground & designed the Indian Map using things readily available on the floor.

Students beautifully designed the physical map of India using material and equipment available on the ground for the PT. Period. They made it more attractive by using coloured stones & sand.

Students were allotted different states for self-study. Students actively participated & gained conceptual insight empowered with theoretical knowledge.

Students exhibited confidence while explaining about states they belong to. It was a fantastic experience for the students & teachers.

• • •

• • •

• • •

• • •

• • •

Story #2

Promila Singh

Gender

Answer: Female

Designation & Name of School or institution

Answer: Self employe/Fashion Deginer/ SOCIALIST

Mobile Number (Whatsapp)

Answer: 9599371633

Write about your Achievement and experience in about 250 words

Answer: Indira Gandhi Award/2018/Award/ congress committee /members2018/Nari sakte award 2019 international woman award/ 2019/

Mrs India world queen award 2018/Golden great icons award 2019/90th gold impress woman award 2019/lifestyle Mazigen show opener 2021/baby fashion show jury 2019/ Delhi kids fashion show jury two times/2021/

guest of honour three times 2019/sarees Sanskrit by Salman sultan show winner 2018/ Socialist award by Dozier newspaper on YouTube 2019/ Rkdx talks core committee members 2021/ Director.

• • •

• • •

• • •

• • •

• • •

• • •

• • •

• • •

• • •

• • •

• • •

Story #3

ARADHANA RANA

Gender

Answer: Female

Designation & Name of School or institution

Answer: DIRECTOR THE ICON PUBLIC SCHOOL

Mobile Number (Whatsapp)

Answer: 8806951250

Write about your Achievement and experience in about 250 words

Answer: MY SUCCESS STORY

Any success story rests on struggles and failures overcome by determination and perseverance; mine is no different! I am a bundle of contradictions in life. I had a childhood that could have broken some, but it evolved me. I studied Nutrition but eventually found my calling in English. I was fiercely career-oriented but found happiness in delving into a hundred things I was not formally qualified for. I lead a life that is looked upon as laid back, but I can't sleep unless I have counted my achievements for the day, and I can't get up from bed unless I have the schedule for the day all planned.

It is a personality defect in me to account for every hour I spend and assure myself that I have utilised it gainfully.

I am almost manic in learning new skills, and despite all the restlessness and the love for good things in life, I can sit for hours writing without any thought of physical comfort!

My journey has been fascinating because I get bored of anything I have mastered! Today, I am a writer, an editor, a designer, a travel blogger, a life coach, a counsellor, a communication skills trainer, and on the way to becoming a publisher—all these skills self-learnt – no professional qualification in any.

The Icon Public School, which I founded in 2008, is now a Senior Secondary CBSE School, is my lifeline; it keeps me ticking! Today, it is a recipient of many awards and honours for innovation in pedagogy because I believe that a motivated team can scale any height. I also think that there is nothing you cannot achieve with perseverance.

• • •

Story #4:

Dr Pramod Kumar Rajput

Gender

Answer: Male

Designation & Name of School or institution

Answer: Vertical head & Sr. Vice President --
Cedilla Pharma Limited, Ahmedabad

Mobile Number (Whatsapp)

Answer: 9979868862

Write about your Achievement and experience
in about 250 words

Answer: Dr Pramod Kumar Rajput is a seasoned corporate professional with a rich experience of over 39years in pharmaceutical & Healthcare, Sales & Marketing while working as Sr. Vice President & Vertical Head in Cadila Pharmaceuticals Limited, an Indian Multinational Leading Pharmaceutical Company based in Ahmedabad

Being an engineering college dropout, he started his professional journey as a Medical Representative and has risen to this position within the same organisation.

He is known as 'The Rajput of Cadila' within the healthcare fraternity. He did his MBA Marketing & Executive Leadership Development Program from IIM, Ahmedabad & is a Member of Leaders Excellence at Harvard Square MLE[SM]*. He also completed his Certification in School Management and Leadership (CSML) from Harvard Business School, Boston, including Diploma in Project Management on Leadership & Team Development, Change Management & Risk Management from International Business Management Institute, Berlin, Germany. He is being nominated as National SDG Ambassador 2021-2030 by UNAccc. He has received 6 Honorary Doctorates in recognition in*

Humanitarian Services, Business Administration, Education, Cultural & Scientific Values, Doctor of Philosophy & Doctorate in Literature (D.Litt.) He also did 24 certification courses from all leading International Universities across the world like Leeds University, London, University of Michigan, (University of Queen's land, Deakin University, CK University) Australia, College of Law, Samsung & Accenture on the various subject including Massachusetts Medical Society & Harvard Medical School USA. He is a Mentor, Change Maker, Moderator, thought leader, active panellist, Chief guest on numerous forums & events. His multiple Podcast on subjects related to Leadership, Journey of life, Attitude & Altitude Perseverance, Growth Mindset, Self -Awareness is featured at many national & a couple of International forum

He has been in the Advisory Board of many Institutions —Mahabodhi Group- Ahmedabad, Poornima University —Jaipur, IES University —Bhopal, LNCT University — Bhopal, Karnavati group of Institutions- Ahmedabad, Sri Venkateswara College of Engineering & Technology (Chittor) AP, Bhavan's College of Pharmacy- Ahmedabad, Modern Group of Institutions, Indore, Mishi group —Delhi, SK Educare- Surat, Sanmadhur group —Delhi, Grab guidance group Delhi, Taringini group,

Bangalore, Q team, Mumbai, Climed Research Solutions, Manipal Karnataka, Positive Thoughts, Regional Director of RDx Talks, Kolkata, Gujarat State – Honorary President of Prithvi Abhuvaday Association India. He is also a part of the International Forum as "Global Ambassador – Commonwealth" of CommonWealth Entrepreneurs Club, UK, Ambassador of Global Mental Health Association (GMHA), USA, Marketing Director of Global Youth Mental Health Awareness (GYMHA); he is representing as an International Influencer on the International Institute of Influencer forum from Oman. He has been given 5 International Awards – One of the Global Mental Health leaders by World Congress of Mental Health Summit, Healthcare Warriors By World Leadership Congress & Awards, International Ambassador of Peace by World Literary Forum for Peace & Human Rights, Global Happiness Olympian award by WHO, Marshal Notre International Award for supporting the Campaign of '" Non-Violence, Femicide, Psychological & Physical Abuse of Women." Inspirational Icon & Global leader by the Global University Intelligence unit has a vision and a great passion for giving back to society. At the same time, keep working through various ways to enhance Learning, Unlearning.

• • •

Story #5: Dr Pallavi Vasudha Vishwas

Dr Pallavi Vasudha Vishwas, nationally and internationally awarded, Founder of Happy Harmony, a Harmony Happiness Coach, Work-life Balance Expert, Inspiring Speaker and Soft Skills Trainer on a mission of Spreading Smiles across Miles ? I help young individuals develop life skills and a growth mindset to ensure they achieve their dreams by enhancing their strengths!

I am passionately empowering busy, ambitious working women to manage stress effectively with a smile and help integrate the work-life to pilot their flight of happiness with self-belief and confidence.

• • •

• • •

• • •

• • •

• • •

• • •

Story #6:

Dr Kalpana Dixit

I have served the education industry for 20 years continuously with a different portfolio. I have started My career- as a JRF to Principal with many awards and recognition. My Experience as an educator is enriching since

it gives the opportunity of becoming part of a person's life and imprint in his mind the knowledge that will allow him to achieve more meaningful goals. It is a two-way process in which both teacher and learner have the opportunity to learn from each other. During my teaching practice, my students taught me that each one knows differently and has a different capacity to process and apply information. Therefore, various activities and methods should be used during class time. When students feel respected and supported by the teacher, they gain confidence and strive when applying new concepts.

This is something that I have seen during my teaching experience with the students and proven to be the same with adults. It is also true that if students can relate the learning to their daily lives, it will be more meaningful and long lasting. Overall, this learning experience has taught me how to treat each student individually but also teach concepts as a whole group. Each student has different needs and although they are all learning the same concept they come to mastery in very different ways. As a future teacher I am thankful this experience has taught me how to help each of my students in the way they need best by incorporating different instructional methods and different ways of learning. I want my classroom to be a place where students' thoughts and ideas are valued and where all voices are heard, in one way or another. I find the emotional environment of a classroom to be extremely important, especially in younger grades, because it can assist students in creating a positive outlook.

• • •

Story #7: Anita Saxena

Anita Saxena is a passionate educationist, freelance Motivational Speaker, a Life Coach & a Neuro-Linguistic Practitioner. She is an Associate Consultant of Education Mentoring India, a one-stop solution for all the school-related issues She believes that she can influence anyone to introspect and find their own goals in life and achieve extreme happiness by achieving them. Being a passionate educationist for three decades, she carries an innate understanding of the behaviour at different age levels. Her expertise in developing rapport with people is a privilege to make anyone share their inconveniences which help her to guide and motivate people to drive their energy calmly in positive efforts to attain the desired outcome. She is fervent to guide and groom students to get to know their strengths and weaknesses, to overcome them and use them for their desired growth. Along with grooming students, she has helped teachers to excel in their profession by not only making their teaching interesting and fun-based, but also guiding them to take their profession to the next level of perfection. She is a certified trainer from the most prestigious training institute, IATD Chennai & a certified Neuro Linguistic Practitioner. Her sessions have been appreciated and acknowledged by the educational institutions and are honoured by their mementoes. She explicates- 'My mission is to be a catalyst in the life of people who dream big for themselves with open eyes.'

• • •

Story #8. Shikha Sharma

The sheen and serene. A microbiologist by education, a nation builder, an entrepreneur, and a Proud Principal who started her career with a humble beginning is today a role model for people in general & women in particular. Her long journey of struggle & achievements is a fascinating story with topsy-tipsy curves & curles. As a nation builder, her contribution finds its recognition through awards like...Best principal of the year by Education Council of India. National award in academic excellence, Acharya chankya shikshavid Samman 2019. As ambassador of women empowerment, she is being associated with La global foundation as ambassador. Another feather in her crown. International progressive women award by Aesthetics established her as a champion of the cause of womenfolk. Her organizational skills and contribution towards the improvement of education & the educational system resulted in awarding her with the Global leadership award by Pscwa & finally appointing her as its State vice president at All private school and children welfare association. She is being associated as Core advisor Haryana at Schoolie. Honorary advisory at sports academy association of India.

• • •

• • •

• • •

Story #9. Dr Meenakshi Narula

Dr Meenakshi Narula is the Principal of Shemford Futuristic K12 School Auraiya. An inspiring academic leader, MIE Master Trainer, MIE Expert, Google Certified Educator-L1, Adobe Creative Educator- Level 2, Mote Certified Educator, Certified Digital Educator, ICT Facilitator Awardee, Global Teachers

Awardee and Rashtriya Shiksha Ratan, Digitized and Most Techno-savvy Principal Awardee, Certified Book Creator Author L-1, and an ardent advocate of technology integration in education and game-based learning.

She is Founder, Director n CEO, Mentoring The Mentors, MSME registered and ISO certified institute (An institute that accelerates your learning curve). She conducts various community outreach programmes to 'Reaching the Unreachable' by conducting workshops and summer programmes for the government school students and teachers. Now as a GEG Leader, Kanpur is looking forward to sharing the knowledge and skills with more educators.

• • •

• • •

• • •

• • •

Story #10. Dr Madhu Ved

Gender Female

Designation & Name of School or institution
Answer: Manager, SBM Sr Sec school Delhi

Mobile Number (whatsapp)
Answer: 9899211336

Write about your Achievement and experience in about 250 words
Answer: Awarded at many prestigious global platforms and NGOs ,with 32 years of diverse experience as Administrator and Principal is constantly on a path to mark a difference in each and every learner within boundaries and beyond .Woods are lovely dark and deep
But I have promises to keep
Miles to go before I sleep
Miles to go before I sleep?♥?

. . .

. . .

. . .

. . .

Story #11. Ms. Jayati Mukherjee

Ms Jayati Mukherjee has been the Chief Editor in several school magazines and recently in online magazines too. She has published a book "REVERIE" in her name where she has shared her thoughts and feelings. She was awarded the Best Teachers award for the highest average in (ENGLISH class XII) board exam (C.B.S.E) amongst all other subjects.

Her students have won the PRESIDENT'S GOLD MEDAL from the premier institution IIT, KHARAGPUR which shows her capability in honing the holistic development of students.

She was the Teacher Coordinator of the Annual-Drama Competition held in BRITISH COUNCIL from where the students gave a commendable performance. She has played an active part in obtaining affiliations in several renowned schools. She has brought several laurels to the schools she has been associated with in the last 26 years. She has the expertise of being the Deputy Centre Coordinator of CTET Exams. During her tenure as Principal in one of the renowned institutions, her school received the 2nd prize in a poster competition on WORLD GIS DAY among eminent schools, where she portrayed the condition of the earth 50 years hence , when trees maybe a rare view if greenery is not saved now. She is a motivational speaker and wants to bring happiness and peace to the lives she touches.

JOURNEY BEHIND THE SUCCESS
MS. JAYATI MUKHERJEE HAS USED HER EXPERIENCE AND KNOWLEDGE FOR BUILDING BRILLIANT INDIVIDUALS. SHE

BELIEVES IN GIFTING BETTER AND FREE HUMAN BEINGS WITH AN INDEPENDENT WILL, TO THE COUNTRY. Ms Jayati Mukherjee has received has received the BEST DISTRICT PRINCIPAL AWARD 2019 -20 BY THE SOF FOUNDATION in recognition of the outstanding performance of her students in MANGALAM VIDYA NIKETAN. Her mission of life is to make everyone realize that there is no shortcut to achieve success, so have faith in yourself because you matter.

• • •

• • •

• • •

• • •

• • •

• • •

• • •

• • •

• • •

• • •

Story #12. Binita Sarkar

This is Binita Sarkar from Kolkata West Bengal from India. I headed the CISCE from Kolkata for about 2 decades and with a small stint of 5 years in Delhi. Now I have started my own eduprenuerial venture, The Centre of Excellence-Kingmakerz of the Future Kolkata, mentoring heads of schools teachers and sharing best educational practices with them.

We have already done more than 30 or more free webinars across India and Abroad with countries like UAE ,UK Australia Singapore and Dubai making an effect on more than 5 lakh educators Heads of Schools teachers at primary secondary and middle school level.

We have partnered and collaborated with many companies e.g VIT business School to establish the brand Image of my company.I have had the privilege and opportunity to Head the CISCE popularly known as the ICSE board having more than thousands of schools across India and other countries. I have won the Rashtriya seva Ratna awards and life time achievement in Eduprenuer and best International Eduprenuer of the year award totally 30 awards to cherish my dream of conducting webinars symposiums meets programmes audio visuals for educators free of cost during the pandemic and won the award from UNDG as one of the best 50 asian women and been featured in a coffee table book also featured as 100 superwoman in India.

• • •

• • •

• • •

Story #13 Sanjana Bakshi Datta

Sanjana Bakshi Datta is a Seasoned education professional with strong leadership, communication, analytical and problem-solving skills. MPhil in Chemistry. Always secured one of top three position in academic career 18 years experience as PGT Chemistry

at DAV Public School, Pushpanjali Enclave Pitampura Delhi 2 years 4 months as head of institution at DAV Public School , R.K. Puram, Delhi

LIFETIME MEMBER: Member of WICCI (Womens Indian Chamber of Commerce and Industry) Lifetime member of CED Foundation, Lifetime member of GTE -INDIA Lifetime member of IAECT (international Association of, Educators and Corporate Trainers), Lifetime member of Vaikalpik chikitsa paddhati vikas sanstha, India, Lifetime membership of RK Quotes speaker forum.

AWARDS RECEIVED: Appointed as Senior Regional Director of RKDx Talks, Conferred with Dynamic Principal of year 2021 by Dr A.P.J. Abdul Kalam Education Excellence Award, Conferred with Acharya Chanakya Shikshavid Samman 2021 for contribution in the field of education and towards the society during pandemic by FUN2LEARN, Conferred with Young Principal of Year 2021 award by Indian Glory Award, Conferred Best Educator Award 2021 by Rhythm Group, Conferred with Dr.Sarvepalli Radhakrishnan International Award of Honour as Young Principal of Year 2021 by Educació World, Honored as one of the Top 100 Iconic Principals by Rhythm Group,

Global Teaching Excellence Award 2021-Young Principal of the year 2021, Global GRKQSF Edutalk's conferred The Best Principal of the year Award 2021, Educació world -Asia Star Rating Award-2021 conferred Young Principal Award 2021 Conferred with title Remarkable Women 2021 by Gajanand Bohra, Dettol conferred with Dettol protector Pack for sharing act of kindness during pandemic, Global Achiever's Award 2021 conferred by All India Radio, Young Principal Of Year 2021 conferred by Asian Education Award, Awarded with Awesome Women Award 2021 by Maan Mahila Ka Awarded with Naari Tu Naranyani Samman 2021 conferred by Fun2learn, Awarded with Mata Surjeet Kaur Virdi Samman 2021, National Excellence Award2020 by Art Production and AIR Aakashwani, Rashtriya Shiksha Rattan 2020 conferred by CED Foundation(News about the award ceremony flashed on Zam Zam TV,JAN TV Rajasthan,IBN News ,Policewala ,Madhya Pradesh Live and various newspapers), Rashtra Prerna Award 2020 by Vaikalpik chikitsa paddhati vikas sanstha, India, SHATAKSHI WOMAN AWARD 2020 by Rhythm Group, National Level Pratibha Samman Golden Peacock Award 2020 by MVLA Trust, Dr. APJ Abdul Kalam International Educator's Honor for Excellence in Education − 2020 conferred by Shree Krishna Educare.The Real Super Women Award 2020 by Forever Star India (Published in newspaper), GLOBAL

TEACHER AWARD 2019, Govt. of India, ZIIEI, Shri Arbindo Educational Society appreciation certificate TEACHER INNOVATION AWARD 2019, SHIKSHA GAURAV NATIONAL TEACHER AWARD 2018, My story being featured as one of the 100 inspiring people in the book 100 Inspiring Indians by DR Tilak Tanwar (Best seller book at Amazon), Acted as Co-Host for webinar conducted by Perfect Health Mela on topic "Mental Health and Well-being"with Dr Reshma Hingorani, Participated as a Speaker in IGA 2021 Conference, Shared my views on K-12 talks 2021 platform on the topic -How coped up with pandemic.

• • •

• • •

• • •

• • •

• • •

• • •

• • •

• • •

• • •

Story #14: Satabdi Roy

Myself Satabdi, an event planner also working as Marketing Head of Kolkata with a National Magazine Vanshdhara. Also working with IBSW as Regional Director of East India and Council Member of WICCI and Member of RTA.Recently got the opportunity to work as Talent Head Manager with United Nation Pageants Ltd & International Business Head of a international channel GNN. Brand model of Minu Saree. Coming to my achievements-

Received William Shakespeare International Award in Poetry, Best Singer Award from Bigframe Films and was also honoured as Celebrity in Lifestyle Magazine. Recieved Nari Shakti Puraskar from NHRO, Brand Face Award in Cricplay Tournament, Received the title of Mrs Goodness Ambassador 2021 and Mrs Glam Queen Fitness 2021. Also received Mrs Top Model India 2021.

• • •

• • •

• • •

• • •

Story #15 Dr. Santhi Saravanan

Dr Santhi Saravanan is the Director of Taru Financial Services by profession, Founder Director of Taru Fine Arts Global Cultural Arts Forum by passion.

She portrays herself in diverse roles as an eminent Entrepreneur, a proficient Artist, a seasoned Motivational Speaker, a veteran Carnatic Musician, a versatile Veena Player, an enthusiastic Writer, an ardent Reader, a skilled Poet, an efficient Sportsperson, and a fanatical Social Activist. She is an avid Painting Artist in Lalit Kala Academy and proves her efficiency by making many world records in art. She has been awarded with honorary doctorates for her excellent art and entrepreneurial skills.

She loves art and culture along with the nature. She shows off her art skills to inculcate the cultural heritage through her artistic works. She is skilled in diverse art forms, specialised in abstract, contemporary art forms. She got various awards, created records and won many titles as an Artist and in all other fields as well.

• • •

• • •

Story #16 Dr Ramesh

Gender
Answer: Male

Designation & Name of School or institution
Answer: Principal, SCAD WORLD SCHOOL

Mobile Number (whatsapp)
Answer: 9843041068

Achievements:

Delivered excellent Social Service at Child Education thereby winning National Award from the Global Achievers, Awarded as Best Social Worker by Pondicherry Students Federation Society in 2005, Best Progressive Principal award by Re-think India, Best School Leader of Tamilnadu – By International Accreditation of India., Best Educational Leader – By Chennai Press organization., Life Time Achievement award by Pondicherry Bar Council., Best School Principal in South India – By IAA., Best Academician award by Educational Research and Development, Dehradun & UK., Best Progressive Principal Award by Centre for Development and Education., Best Principal of the year 2017 – AKS world Service., Sardar Vallabhbhai Patel national Reformer Award from IRDP Journals, Best Visionary Leader of India International Award by Ink Edu Media Award, Life Time Achievement award – By International Global Peace University, Best Principal of the year 2019 – International award in Bangkok, Best Principal of the year 2020 by Institute of Scholars, Asia's greatest Principal in the year 2020-21 by Humming Bird Education Ltd.,

Youngest Youth Principal awarded by Dr Abdul Kalam Foundation.

• • •

Story #17 Mr Vinay Kumar Jha

Achievements: He is a senior Principal with many years of experience currently working at Pt. Salagram School, Greater Noida, Uttar Pradesh, India. A dynamic educator by choice who believes in learning to learn as a hobby.

Mr. V.K. Jha is a testimony in himself towards dedication and leading a team of teachers and students and has been a known figure in the field of education. His innovative and creative ideas explore at his workplace and speak for his skills and leadership in practice.

• • •

• • •

• • •

• • •

• • •

• • •

• • •

• • •

• • •

Story #18: *RANJAN KUMAR PATTANAYAK*

Ranjan Kumar Pattanayak

Achievements: As a High School Principal, Academic Manager, Dean and Head of Education, Mr. Ranjan is a quality educator with traits towards being a wow academician in practice. With more than 20 years of experience as a High School Principal, Zonal Academic Manager, Founder/Director with expertise in allocating and managing resources in educational organizations. Extensive knowledge of academic standards, in districts as well as state, and local regulations.

Budget-conscious and goal-driven with demonstrated success in implementing programs to boost academic achievement. A dedicated educator by choice and open to learning and taking risk towards success in life.

• • •

• • •

• • •

• • •

• • •

• • •

• • •

• • •

• • •

...

Story 19:

Dr. Vedavathi Dinesh

Achievements: Dr Veddavathi Dinesh is a strong believer of "Simple Living and High Thinking", A personality who is a Passionate Educator, completed her studies in a Government school and college with a law background hails from rural parts of Bengaluru where people only think that the quality education is only meant for so- called "Highly profiled People" gave birth to GREEN EDEN PUBLIC SCHOOL with a strong motive that Quality also can reach to "Low profiled People" without making any difference.

She has more than 15 years of experience in the teaching field and 5 years of experience as a Founder principal observed many obstacles in bridging a gap between education students parents and institutions, but the common and important factor which connects everyone and everything is finance barrier, most of the parents can overcome it but try to compensate and convince themselves with the education what they afford for their children. A dedicated educator with great commitment and loyalty to her workplace.

• • •

• • •

• • •

• • •

Story #20 Shanoli Ray

Achievements: I'm an advocate of growth and innovation in the management of educational organizations with a professional experience of 20 years and 5 years as Principal. I commenced my teaching career as a lecturer for Fashion Design, INIFD in 2000. Spent the next 16 years teaching a wide array of institutes, both

CBSE AND ICSE, strategizing new ways to modernize the learning culture. Being designated as Principal, I have worked on cultivating a healthy relationship among all the stakeholders involved, which helped in overall growth and development of the organisation as well as increase in the student strength. I believe in creating a school environment that embraces a clear and shared focus, high levels of communication , collaboration and respect for diversity.

While framing the curriculum, I try to apply various linguistic, auditory, visual and kinesthetic methods to make learning fun and effective. I try to instill the passion for learning, inquisitiveness and expansion of mind among my students and instigate monitored freedom of thought and expression among students to bring out the best in them. My present school, located in rural Bengal, is being awarded as MOST CREATIVE SCHOOL, 2021. Being the Founding Principal, I emphasized on designing, developing and implementing a curriculum that's appropriate for the overall holistic development of the rural children. Empowerment of the staffs is one of my main focus as an administrator.

I emphasize on Macro management and timely delegation. My adaptability, effective communication, quick decision making ability , pleasing personality and empathetic nature plays a vital role in smooth running of the organization. I'm a keen follower of lifelong learning, personal and professional development through continuous research and timely implementation. Apart from a thorough professional, I'm associated with some NGOs like CRY, Social Development International(SODEIT), Child Chapter India, Women of Heart, UK as Honorary Advisor and Volunteer, sharing my knowledge, expertise and skills for empowerment of women and children. I'm a frequent traveler, photographer and blogger too.

• • •

• • •

• • •

• • •

• • •

• • •

• • •

• • •

Story #21 Ila Upadhyaya

Achievements: Ila is a Principal AGPS Pahalgam (J&K). A motivational speaker, educator, poetess and a sportsperson at heart.

Having teaching experience in various Army Schools in India . My motto is to inspire and motivate the students to be positive in every situation in life and work hard to achieve their goals and be a good human being.

Story #22 Tharanirajan. G

Tharanirajan.   G   EDUCATIONIST, PSYCHOLOGIST

M. Sc, M. A., B. Ed.. PGDCA
Director : INSIGHT LIVES (A place to enlighten the lives)

Achievements: Being a mastery in Psychology, Mr. Tharanirajan has nurtuted a lot of changes in the minds of many youths of the society today. With his proficient achievements as an educationalist layed the foundations to excel as a psychologist, that has assisted hundreds of mentally disturbed students, youngsters, professionals and patients. He is also empathetic profesional making him to understand his patients' feelings and establishing a strong rapport with them. He Provided multi-disciplinary and evidence-based therapies to aid positive behavioral changes in the classroom, at home and in the community. He was evident with his adage which did not stop him from supporting and comforting his patients as well as many students even when the world shut down during the COVID 19 lockdown.

By taking his successful steps as an Author, his first book entitled "Paesum Paena" focused on the betterment of millennials and their parents who can't imagine a world without the internet. As a mentor, he published his second book "Catalyst Chemistry" that made Chemistry an effortless subject to the CBSE students of class

12. He has also penned several articles for newspapers that discusses about the mental well being student relationship and other societal concerns. Being a considerate person of the lives of many rural and uneducated children, he is paralleley tutoring them with basic knowledge and skills of his locality. And he has been awarded Dr. APJ award, Best teacher award, Aacharya chanakya etc for his contribution to the education society.

• • •

• • •

• • •

• • •

• • •

• • •

• • •

• • •

• • •

• • •

Story #23: Kousik Biswas

Achievements: Kousik Biswas was born into a small mediocre family in Chakradharpur, Jharkhand, India. His father, Shri Gour Gopal

Biswas was a railway employee posted in Chakradharpur. His mother, Shrimati Supra Biswas is a housewife.

Kousik completed his school, college in Chakradharpur, and did his M.A. in English literature from the Indira Gandhi National Open University, New Delhi. Currently, he is the Vice-Principal of a leading residential-cum day school in North-East India. He is also a "Visharad" in "Tabla"

Mr. Kousik is basically an "English Teacher". He was a "Teacher" of "English Literature" in "Bishop Westcott School, Khunti, Ranchi, Jharkhand", which is one of the best boarding-cum-day schools in Jharkhand, affiliated to the CISCE, New-Delhi. Thereafter he was fortunate to join "Delhi Public School, Panipat Refinery, Panipat, Haryana". He is an expert in teaching "English Literature" of the CISCE (Classes IX to XII).

• • •

• • •

• • •

Story #24 DR.BALACHANDER

Achievements: DR.BALACHANDER is a renowned educator of India. Acting DIRECTOR- of RKDx TALKS, India. An EDUCATIONIST, Dr Balachander is a known educator with expertise of school leadership

and classroom management. As a resource and a CERTIFIED LEADERSHIP & CAREER COACH he has also been involved in many workshops as a resource person. He is also a RENOWNED PANELIST AT NATIONAL EDULEADERS SUMMIT and has been deliberating as a wonderful SPEAKER AT INTERNATIONAL FORUM ON EDUCATIONAL FRONTS PAN India.

• • •

• • •

• • •

• • •

• • •

• • •

• • •

• • •

• • •

• • •

• • •

Story #25 Saloni Galundia

Saloni Galundia

Gender: Female

*Designation & Name of School or institution
Answer: Head of operation, Jain public school*

a part of jain group of institutions, Bangalore: Mobile Number (whatsapp) 7427008898

Achievements: Saloni Galundia is a Educator, Trainer, consultant, social activist and life couch. As a lawyer, pursuing PhD and did MBA from delhi her career as PRO while doing her MBA from Delhi. While doing her summer internship was offered the job in Jain group of institutions as a head of operation for madhya pradesh .she started her 3 k12 school and 3 pre primary school in madhya pradesh with motive to provide education to the places where their was scarity and requirement of good educational institutions with that in mind started the school in barnagar,ratlam and jhabua.A small town where the education was not a privilege and need of the hour .She even got various awards and nomination, which include, maharana pratap bravery, RKDx talk special award for best influencer, green award for best leader, Dr APJ abdul Kalam international award for excellence, nayaka award from nae duniya. She has also had tied with various education departments of various countries and has organized trips for school leaders for their learning along with this she is also actively associated with various people as a social worker.

• • •

Story #26: Nikita Bagle

Nikita Bagle has total 15yrs of experience as a lecturer, and working as a PGT. She is a passionate educator who's committed towards sharing her expertise, creativity and superior instructional strategies has led her to win laurels in the field of Education. Mrs. Nikita Bagle has completed her M.Com in Financial Accounting and B.Ed, with core subject as Commerce and Economics. She has also completed her training and Certified in *different areas and achieved success. Such as:-* **AREA OF *STOCK EXCHANGE* She is** *AMFI Certified, CAPITAL MARKET Certified, DERTIVATIVE MARKET Certified. She is training senior level students to invest in paper currency, imparting the value and importance of investment at earlier stage.* **AREA OF *EDUCATION AND SKILLS TRANING*,** *A Certified NLP trainer from National Institute of Skills Training. A CERTIFIED MASTER TRAINER from National Institute of Skills Training and from GLOBAL TALK EDUCATION FOUNDATION. A CERTIFIED STOTY TELLER from National Institute of Skills Training Institute. A CERTIFIED MASTER TRANER ON SCHOOL LEADER AND PADAGOGY FROM GLOBAL TALK EDUCATION FOUNDATION. Training completed in TECHNOLOGY BLENDED LEARNING. Training completed in EDUCATION FOR PEACE. Training completed in PERSPECTIVE BUILDING ON LIFE SKILLS. Mrs. Nikita Bagle is a Professional trainer of rich history of contributing training expertise in promoting professional excellence across diverse functional disciplines.*

She has demonstrated matured professional grip in designing & delivering high impact training modules catering to the specialized needs of individuals. With extraordinary personality development, public speaking,

Interpersonal skills, behavioral and investing skills as a major. She has conducted 12 workshops in last 3 months for many individual. She is an electrifying speaker and can motivate and activate humans with her unique style. She trains in a way which engages and leaves the people spell bound. She has mastery in bringing out the best in every human being through her trainings, motivational speaking, coaching and also key note speaking. She has proven competencies in application of modernized training methodology to generate far reaching impact on the psyche of all levels of participants and liberate the hidden human potential.

• • •

• • •

• • •

• • •

• • •

• • •

• • •

Story #27: Dr Ushavati Shetty

Dr Ushavati Shetty is an Energetic and innovative teaching professional with the ability to bring lessons to life and cultivate an eager and active classroom bringing knowledge of teaching science in order to engender critical thinking skills in students which will make them understand how the world around them works.

Talent for developing well balanced lesson plans that teach the fundamentals, enhance students' academic skills and prepare them for assessments.

Incorporate experiments, technology and visual representations and offer extracurricular help to make certain that each student is able to grasp the materials and concepts in whichever manner suits him/her best. Possess exceptional leadership skills to foster strong relationship with students and colleagues. A Principal at **Navodaya English High School & Jr. College, Thane, she is an energetic and a vibrant educator with learning as a priority for life.**

• • •

• • •

• • •

• • •

• • •

• • •

• • •

Story # 28: Mohan Thakur

Mohan Thakur comes from from Dehradun, Uttaralhand, India. He has done his Graduation with English Honours, MA in English, LL.B., B.ed. in English and is having 17+ years experiences including 6years as a

Principal in CBSE affiliated school. A MotivationalSpeaker and Certificate NLP PRACTIONER, by choice is a great contributer in the field of academics at large.

• • •

About The Authors

Dr Dheeraj Mehrotra

www.authordheerajmehrotra.comAn Educator,
Author, Innovator, LIMCA Book Record Holder, Premium

UDEMY Instructor, National Awardee, Dr Dheeraj Mehrotra is a dedicated individual. He secures experience as an Author, School Principal, Teacher, School Academic Auditor, Teacher Trainer and a CBSE Resource. He received the Best Teacher Award from the President of India in the Year, 2006 and the Best Science Teacher Award by the Ministry of Science and Technology, State of UP. Authored over 100 books (Available on Amazon), developed over 450 Educational Courses on UDEMY.COM catering to over Seven Lakh Students from 180 plus countries. Presently he is the Principal at Kunwar's Global School, Lucknow, India.

• • •

• • •

• • •

• • •

• • •

• • •

• • •

• • •

• • •

Dr R K Das

RK Das is a Founder & Chairman of GLOBAL RK QUOTES SPEAKERS FORUM, Inspirational Speaker, writer and author of RK Quotes. RK Das is the Managing Director of GRKQSF EDUTALKS unit of GRKQSF registered under the Ministry of MSME, Govt of India. Global RK Quotes Speakers Forum is an ISO 9001:2015 Certified. He is a creator of RK Das motivational videos. He has vast knowledge in the field of teaching and administration as a lecturer in college and Principal in CBSE affiliated schools. He trained more than 120 teachers about digital learning. He is also expertise in online CBSE Affiliation work. He holds a Master degree in Commerce, Accountancy and management. He possesses extensive and rich experience of 27 years in teaching and administration. He is rewarded as Global Eduleader 2020 by CED-India. His work spans the areas of inspirational and motivational quotes writer & speaker. He also conducts seminars, workshops and other online events at GRKQSF EDUTALKS.

www.ingramcontent.com/pod-product-compliance
Lightning Source LLC
Chambersburg PA
CBHW072118150726
47999CB00005B/2026